How to Sell on Etsy

With Pinterest

Selling on Etsy Made Ridiculously

Easy Vol.2

by Charles Huff

Founder, Craft Biz Insider

Published in USA by: Craft Biz Insider

Charles Huff

© Copyright 2018

ISBN-13: 978-1-970119-20-6

ISBN-10: 1-970119-20-9

Table of Contents

Also By Charles Huff

How to Sell on Etsy With Facebook

How to Sell on Etsy With Blogging

How to Sell on Etsy With Instagram

About the Author

Charles Huff is a former cubicle drone turned full-time Etsy seller.

He is also the owner of the world's most neurotic Jack Russell Terrier.

A Special FREE Gift for You!

If you'd like FREE instant access to my special report "Top 10 Marketing Tools Every Etsy Seller Should Use" then head over to **CraftBizInsider.com/Free**.

(What else you gonna do? Watch another "Twilight" movie?!)

Prologue: Why Pinterest is So Freakin' Awesome for Us Etsy Sellers

"Anyone who has never made a mistake has never tried anything new."

-Albert Einstein

I LOVE Pinterest.

You should see the looks I get from my guy friends when I mention that little tidbit.

And not because I'm looking for new ways to decorate my bathroom — shabby chic! — or trying to find that inspirational quote that'll help me get through another Monday.

Or Tuesday.

No, I love Pinterest because it makes me money. (And I like things that make me money, especially with little effort.)

Reasons are simple:

- Pinterest users are buyers (They pin stuff they want all day long.)

- Pinterest users are buyers of things that aren't cheap (They spend nearly double what Facebook and Twitter users spend, combined.)

- Pinterest users like things that can be expressed visually.

- Pinterest users like things creative, artistic, individual, aspirational….

And luckily for us ALL of those things describe the artisanal goodness we offer over at our Etsy store. (Or through other platforms.)

I don't care if you sell decorative brass knuckles or organic aloe vera toothpaste...(is that thing?)

If you aren't marketing on Pinterest, then you are leaving serious money on that handmade Etsy table.

Now, this doesn't mean it's easy. Or simple. Or it happens overnight.

You might have tried Pinterest in the past. You may even be on there right now.

You may pin each day to your heart's content, and not sure why the only followers you've got share your last name.

I've been there.

I tried Pinterest many times before I figured out that it might be a good idea if I did read and paid attention to what other people were doing successfully on Pinterest so I could have a vague notion of what the heck I was doing.

Once I figured out what worked and what didn't — and got over my male prejudice of all things Pinterest — I learned that Pinterest is easy, effective, and perfect for us Etsy sellers.

But you gotta have a system. And that's what I will share with you in this book.

So fasten that hand-woven seat belt, we're about to take your Etsy business, and your Pinterest presence, to a level you never thought possible.

Chapter 1:

A Beginner's Guide to

Pinterest

"When you know better, you do better."

-Maya Angelou

As much as I love Pinterest — and I might be one of the few guys who do — getting up and running on this Uber-popular social network can be a challenge.

Especially when all their terminology seems like it was named by an over-caffeinated 12-year-old.

So, before we get into all that delicious pinning that can drive serious traffic back to your website, Etsy store, Facebook page or wherever you like…

Let's do a super-brief refresher course to make

sure we all know our pins from our pinboards.

Confusing Pinterest Term No.1: The Pin

The pin is a term for the action Pinterest users take to share images or videos they like.

They call them "pins," because these pins live in themed collections called "boards" or "pinboards." (More on those later.)

There are four ways for a Pinterest user to "pin" something. And that is:

1. Pinning an item using a "Pin It" button on the website that contains the image or video.
2. Pinning the item with the Pinterest bookmarklet installed on the user's browser.
3. Uploading the image or video to Pinterest.
4. Pasting the URL of the web address into their Pinterest dashboard (and having Pinterest "find" the image or video they'd like to share.)

In my Pinterest experience, the first method is by far the most common way Pinterest users share stuff they like.

I find most people just won't go to the trouble of uploading images or installing anything as strangely named as a bookmarklet.

Still, it's important to remember you are a Pinterest user too, so make sure to "pin" all of your own Etsy product photos, regardless of how the rest of the Pinterest community is engaging with your photos and videos.

The text description, or caption, of each pin provides a fantastic opportunity to include price information, popular keywords and links back to your site or Etsy store.

Cool, huh?

Confusing Pinterest Term No.2: The Repin

The repin used to be a HUGE part of the Pinterest ecosystem. It refers to when a user "pins" something that a Pinterest user has ALREADY pinned.

Pinterest has tried its best to phase out the "repin" term — removing it from its hover icons, perhaps to avoid confusion with "regular" pins.

Hard to say what Pinterest has planned for the future; like Facebook they may end up changing their policy every 15 minutes.

But for now ALL pins, whether they be original or repins of other people's stuff we will call "pins."

Note: 80% of all "pins" are, in fact, "repins." This means original content is very much the exception to the rule.

Confusing Pinterest Term No.3: The Like

These are akin to the more famous Facebook "like" — but instead of using the more traditional thumbs-up icon, Pinterest likes are designated, at least as of the writing of this book, by a heart symbol.

Pinterest likes require a lot less time and/or effort than pins; users don't have to provide a caption or select a pinboard for the "like" to live in. They click the heart icon, and they've given their approval of a certain pin.

Pinterest likes aren't as powerful as a pin or repin. But recent research suggests that a pin's number of likes DOES boost its visibility in the Pinterest universe.

"Anything Else?"

Nope, that's pretty much it. Once you get the concept of each user having an unlimited number of pinboards, with which they populate with an unlimited amount of pins, then you're more than halfway to conquering this whole Pinterest marketing thing.

The only thing left to do will be to create an awesome Pinterest profile that'll boost your chances of getting found and making some Etsy store sales. And that's what we will cover in the next chapter.

Chapter 2:

Creating a Cool Pinterest Account

"Life isn't about finding yourself. It's about creating yourself."

-George Bernard Shaw

I have to warn you before we get started, Pinterest does not make it easy.

For a social network so aligned with the same creative energies that drew us Etsy sellers to our creative business, they seem to make it quite confusing — and technical — to create a Pinterest business account.

Just so you know, the steps we will cover in this chapter will be technical and might make you feel you're repeating 9th-grade Algebra. (For the third time.)

But worry not as soon as we get through the Dark Forest of Pinterest Account Creation we'll be on to greener — and much more interesting — pastures.

So, here are my 4 Steps to Creating a Pinterest Business Profile That Totally Rocks:

Pinterest Profile Step No.1: Create a Business Profile

I know a lot of Etsians continue to do all of their Pinterest marketing with "regular" consumer Pinterest accounts. This is a mistake because:

- There's a heck of a lot more you can do with a Pinterest business profile.
- Marketing your wares with a personal profile violates Pinterest's terms of service.

Though I know nobody who has had their

Pinterest account closed down to hawking their new product line, I think as Pinterest grows — just as happened with Facebook — they will get increasingly stringent with their guidelines.

But the biggest reason to have a business account is that you can set the name of your profile to your business — something you can't do with a personal account.

So, that being said, here's how you do it:

- Visit http://business.pinterest.com.
- Select the *"Join as a Business"* option.
- Insert your company info (You'll want to check that an account hasn't already been created with your business name).
- If you can add a keyword, such as "decorative candles" or "vintage decor," get it in there.

Presto! You've got a Pinterest business account. The next step is perhaps the most complicated which is…

Pinterest Profile Step No.2: Verify That Website of Yours

Okay, take a breath. Because we're about to jump into the fascinating world of HTML and meta verification.

Told ya it was going to get tech-y.

Here's the deal, Pinterest wants to make ABSOLUTELY SURE your business account is tied to an actual business. An issue that has plagued Twitter for years.

And the way Pinterest can ensure you aren't some Russian hacker is to have you:

1) Upload a small (invisible) HTML file to the server of your website.

Or…

2) Add a meta tag (just a piece of code) to the home page of your website.

Now both are simple — if you're comfortable with things like FTP (File Transfer Protocol) and adding bits of code to the <head> tag of your home page.

If what I said sounds like a line of dialogue from a Transformers movie, then my wholehearted recommendation would be to head over to a site like Upwork or Fiverr and hire somebody SUPER CHEAP to do this for you.

At Upwork or Fiverr you can find a talented, but unemployed, freelancers all over the world who can handle this for you in five minutes. (For as little as $5-$10.)

Pinterest Profile Step No.3: Fill Your Profile With Etsy Goodness

This is where a lot of Etsians miss a real opportunity with their Pinterest profile, and that is outfitting their Pinterest profile real estate for maximum impact.

Here's what I would do:

1. **Add a brief description of your Etsy store in the "About Me" section of your**

Pinterest profile. Keep it brief but make it emotional and personal. Instead of writing: "Woodsy Creations specializes in handmade cabinetry"…try something like…"Woodsy Creations is a husband-and-wife artisan team who create a wonderful, handmade kitchen cabinetry guaranteed to delight and wonder."

2. **Get keywords in your "about me" description**. You don't have to go overboard with this, but again notice how I got "handmade kitchen cabinetry" in there, without seeming too obvious. Plug them in, as long as they make sense.

3. **Link up your Facebook and Twitter accounts, to your Pinterest accounts**. Now this assumes your Facebook and Twitter accounts are focused on your Etsy business, not pictures of your 12-year-old on a water ski.

4. **Turn off the "Search privacy" settings on your account**. This SHOULD be turned off

by default, but you want to make sure under "Account settings" that you don't have this feature enabled. Doing so will cause your profile to be undiscoverable in the Pinterest and external search engines. No bueno.

Pinterest Profile Step No.4: Connect Your Pinterest Profile and Your Etsy Shop

Though you can't technically reproduce your Etsy store in its entirety on your Pinterest account – wouldn't that be nice? – you can connect the two so that:

- People on Etsy that see your stuff have an easier time connecting with you on Pinterest
- People on Pinterest that see your stuff have an easier time connecting with you on Etsy

Does this mean you'll INSTANTLY get thousands of new customers by syncing these two up?

No. You'll still have to do the strategies outlined in this book. (Sorry.)

But you'll remove as many obstacles between a total stranger becoming a potential customer and a lifelong customer.

Setting this up in the back-end of your Etsy store is pretty simple. You just:

- Login to your Etsy store
- Head over to "Shop Manager" – it has the icon that looks like car on top of a swimming pool (God knows why)
- Click on the "Marketing" tab on the far left of the dashboard
- Choose "Social Media"
- Decide on which social media networks you will connect with your Etsy store

You have the option of four platforms: Pinterest, Facebook (you specify the page), Instagram or Twitter.

I recommend you do as many as you feel

comfortable connecting. But, obviously, in this tome we are concerned with Pinterest.

Warning: Be careful when connecting, if you have multiple Pinterest accounts, that you expand the login window as big as possible. Otherwise you might connect the wrong account. (Like I did.)

Pinterest Profile Step No.4: Upload a GREAT (Optimized) Profile Photo

We're in the home stretch now. All that's left is to upload an awesome profile photo and you're good to go!

Except...

Most Pinterest profile photos are — how can I say this nicely? — as interesting as a tax seminar. Which is a shame because this is the MOST consistent visual part of your profile.

So, here are a few things I've learned the hard way about finding a great Pinterest profile photo:

- **Unless your logo is great, don't use it**. I

find most people don't connect emotionally to a logo. (Unless it's recognizable or awesome.)

- **Pictures of YOU work best!** Forget the stock photo of that anorexic female model smiling awkwardly. Give us your personality in the profile photo.

- **Pictures of YOU working on your craft work even better!** Get a shot of you in your craft room or work area. (Tip: get a friend or colleague, with some photo experience, to take it for you.

- **Make sure the photo looks good when cropped to a square.** Otherwise it'll look odd.

- **Have the photo cropped to 165x165.** If you don't know how to do this, you can hire somebody on Upwork to do it for you. Or the cool, FREE tool PicMonkey also works great.

- **Before uploading the photo, rename it**

with a keyword. Instead of naming your photo "DollCompany_1"…instead go for…"Vintage Dollhouses - Doll Company" to get extra keyword awesomeness in there.

And that's it! Do those five steps, and you'll be way ahead of 90% of the other Pinterest users out there. All we need to do now is create awesome pin-worthy content. (Which is what we'll cover in the next chapter.)

Chapter 2 Action Steps:

- **Go business class**. Create a Pinterest business account. Try to work a keyword into your Pinterest name if you can. But don't force it.

- **Verify your website by uploading code to your site**. If in doubt, hire somebody at a site like Upwork to take it off your plate.

- **Fill out the rest of your profile with keywords and other goodies**. Focus on the "About Me" section — don't forget to link your Facebook and Twitter accounts to your Pinterest accounts.

Create an awesome, snazzy profile photo that includes YOU doing something crafty. Make sure it's cropped to 165x165 and that the photo file name has keywords in it.

Chapter 3: The Ultimate Pinterest Content Toolbox

"When words become unclear, I focus with photographs."
-Ansel Adams

Even Pinterest newbies know the social network runs on one premium grade of fuel: pictures…and lots of 'em.

Other notable social platforms, such as Facebook and Twitter, offer an array of content that INCLUDES pictures.

But everything we want to do on Pinterest:

- Get people to pin our content
- Get more subscribers to our email list
- Send more people to our Etsy store
- Sell more glorious stuff

Revolves around our ability to capture the magic, the emotion — and the artistry — of our Etsy business with pictures.

Posting fuzzy, grainy, and boring photos — that don't tell people what to do…such as "pinning" our photos — won't cut it.

So that's what we will cover in this chapter. I will let you take a peek behind the curtain at the tricks and tools power Pinterest marketers use to not only create and upload fantastic-looking images…

But also how to ensure those images get shared, pinned and lead to additional sales.

Pinterest Tool No.1: A Basic Understanding of Light and Camera-ship

Huh? How is an understanding of light and camera-ship a tool?

Well, even using the most expensive DSLR camera on the market — and they can get expensive — won't help you take awesome pictures, if you don't comprehend that good photos are all about a light source.

See, cameras today are almost TOO GOOD at capturing all the information coming into their lens.

Often, they don't know what to focus on, what to illuminate and what not to illuminate, so you end up with photos that are often grainy, under- or over-exposed and just look rather junky online.

Here are basic rules I follow when taking pictures of my products to get them ready for Pinterest prime-time:

- **Always keep the light to your back**. You want the light source to be shining on the object, not toward the camera.
- **Natural light always looks best**. If you can put your products on an outdoor picnic table, it can make them look cool. (And give them a warm, natural feel.)
- **Mornings and late afternoons are good for shooting**. You want the sun at an angle.

Not right overhead. (Noontime is the worst time to shoot outside.)

- **If you're shooting inside, try to get some additional light behind you**. No matter how much light you think you've got inside, you'll want more.

- **Contrary to popular belief, light doesn't have to be even on both sides**. Shadows can look kinda cool on your Etsy products. You'll want to play with it to see what looks best for your stuff.

- **Be sure to tap or focus on the primary object in the photo before shooting**. This lets the camera know who the heck the main character is in the photo.

- **Take a breath, exhale, then shoot**. I know this seems weird, but people, me included, hold our breath while shooting a photo. This can lead to sudden jerking and bad focus.

Pinterest Tool No.2: A Tripod

Notice I haven't said a thing about whether to take pictures with your Canon Vixia 5400 or the smartphone sitting in your pocket.

That's because I don't think it matters a huge amount; awesome photos can be taken with your iPhone or Android phone of your choice.

But it's vital you invest in some kind of tripod, no matter what kind of device you use to take your pictures.

This is because modern camera lenses are as sensitive as a tween girl reading Twilight and they interpret any slight movement or change.

And no matter how still and stationary you think you are, you are still moving somewhat.

Smartphone tripods are good if you plan to do most of your shooting that way. I like the Charger City line of tripods - they're cheap, they're (fairly) sturdy, and they get the job done.

If you're looking for a beefier tripod, that'll hold a digital camera or one of those HUGE DSLR's, then you'll need something in the $75-$100 range.

Don't buy the ultra-expensive tripods. You don't need 'em.

Pinterest Tool No.3: PicMonkey Editing Platform

So, no matter how great a picture you take you will need some kind of editing interface to do things such as:

- Resize your photos
- Adding CTA (call-to-action) text (such as "Share the love by pinning this image").
- Adding cool effects, such as sepia tone or nifty tints
- Cleaning up your photos (by adjusting saturation and brightness levels)

While you might have great photo editing software already — I'm still trying to figure out how my copy of Photoshop works — my wholehearted recommendation is a tool that is powerful, easy-to-use, and is TOTALLY free.

It's called PicMonkey, it's a virtual editor — meaning you don't have to download any software. And you can do a ton of cool, creative things with your photos on PicMonkey.

It's like they designed it for us Etsy sellers in mind.

Now, there are some advanced features which you must pay for — I think my membership comes out to about three dollars a month. But this one tool alone has skyrocketed my success on Pinterest and has boosted sales on my Etsy shop.

Pinterest Tool No.4: A Willingness to Put Yourself in Photos

I know what you're thinking: it should be about your creations. Why do I have to BE in the pictures?

But we Etsy sellers are ALSO storytellers.

And the story you're telling with your Etsy

store is a compelling one that captivates every customer we have: it's possible to make money doing something you love.

So, if you're shy in front of the camera, try your best to resist the urge to run screaming for the hills when somebody approaches with a camera.

Some of the best, and most shared, photos I've put on Pinterest are me and my mom slaving away in the old craft room. (And trust me, I'm no Brad Pitt.)

Pinterest Tool No.5: A Blog or Website (Optional)

Now this isn't required, and you don't HAVE to have a blog or website to run a successful Pinterest marketing campaign for your Etsy store.

But I like having my own blog as an Etsy seller because:

- They're easy to run
- They're free
- I can place all my Pinterest-worthy photos

there

- Google likes 'em (This one alone should inspire you to create one)
- It's Internet real estate I own

It's that last part I LOVE most of all.

If you want to put an email sign-up on the sidebar of your blog, right next to all those awesome Pinterest-worthy photos, then you can do it.

If you want to have an Etsy shopping cart of your latest creations right above your photos, you can do it. (These are things you can't do with a Facebook Fan Page or Etsy store.)

It's beyond this book to cover setting up a blog, but there are quite a few resources out there — including some fabulous books on Amazon — about how to set up a WordPress blog to become a hub for your Pinterest photo archive.

Just remember, my 72-year-old mom can run a blog. (And this is a lady who still has an AOL email.)

Chapter 3 Action Steps:

- **Grasp that good photos are about good lighting, not an expensive camera**. Try to shoot outdoors as much as you can and keep the light behind the camera, shining toward the subject.

- **Invest in a tripod**. Don't need to spend a lot, but it will help produce crisp, clear images.

- **Get a PicMonkey account**. It's an awesome FREE tool that lets you clean up images and add cool text overlays (that encourage users to "pin" your pictures).

- **Resolve to put yourself in the pictures you pin**. People don't want just products. They want YOU!

- **Set up a blog if you don't already have one**. This will make promoting images easier, and it can bring in some added traffic to your Etsy store.

Chapter 4:

How to Become a PinBoard Expert

"Repeat the good. And the bad. Do it all, and pile on the years."

-Natsuki Takaya

Many people think it's "pins" that make the Pinterest world go round. But it's in the "boards" that house those "pins" where all the Pinterest magic happens.

Because Pinterest boards let you:

- Organize your content by theme
- Target customers
- Feature different areas of your product line

- Feature different price points of your product line
- Feature product bundles and holiday-themed specials (These are popular)
- Recognize your customers and/or Etsy store team
- Tell many compelling, visual stories (Alienating no segment of your customer base.)

So, before we dig into the deep end of the "pin" pool, we will lay the foundation for all your Pinterest marketing success, by creating some awesome pin boards that encourage and boost your bottom line.

Step No.1: Brainstorm Pinboard Ideas

So what boards should we create as Etsy sellers? Well...whatever boards we like!

If you come up with a cool, interesting idea for a board — I once saw a board called "Things to Wear to Your High School Reunion" — then by all means create it!

That being said, there's nothing sadder than a lonely Pinterest board with just two or three pins. (Something I used to create with some regularity.)

So, here are a couple of Pinterest boards I think every Etsy seller should have (at the minimum):

- **A board for each product category.** Example: Kitchen, Outdoor, Victorian, etc.

- **A board for any relevant holiday themes.** Example: Christmas, Halloween, Arbor Day, etc.

- **A "New and Noteworthy" board.** This lets people know about what you'll have coming out of the craft room soon.

- **A Testimonial board.** Here's where you can post all those awesome comments you've gotten from your customers.

- **A "Customer Spotlight" board** Call attention to one of your fave customers - these work like gangbusters.

- **A "Behind-the-Scenes" board.** Give folks a look at your work environment - people love these.

- **A "Special Offer" board.** Feature any discounts or sales you've got going on.
- **A "How-To/Tutorial" board.** These are great for showing people how you make the awesome things you do (without giving up trade secrets).

Now, you could, and should, create more than this if you feel so inclined. But these are a good start and will keep your Pinterest community engaged for quite some time.

Step No.2: Create (and Name) Your Boards

So, creating the boards is pretty dang easy. All you do is select the "Add+" button in the upper right of your Pinterest dashboard, and click on "create a board."

The real art to Pinterest board creation is in naming the darn things. Here are a couple guidelines in using this valuable Pinterest real estate:

- **Go beyond the generic**. Most boards are named like the person was on Valium. Have fun. Take a chance. Don't do: "Bathroom Pot-pourri Ideas"…instead do: "When Bathroom Pot-pourri Attacks."

- **Keywords matter…a lot**. You don't want to go crazy here but try to weave in those ever-magical keywords into the board names whenever you can. (But be subtle. You are trying to reach human eyeballs.)

- **If keywords have got you stumped, then just add a modifier at the end**. When I have no idea what to name my boards, I try to add words like "creations," "gifts," "stories," or "magic" to the end of a keyword. (Example: Handmade Lavender Soap Magic; Vintage Victorian Doll Creations.)

- **You're not married to your board name**. You can change it any time. (Just realize that each time you change the board name, the URL changes, so you must update your promotional links.)

Step No.3: Divide and Conquer

So, chances are, if you're an Etsy seller, you're in charge of many aspects of your Etsy business. The:

- Product design
- Product creation
- Marketing
- Sales
- IT
- …Everything!

Which is understandable, I mean none of us Etsy sellers grow up with "Rockefeller" in our last name. And you may well plan on managing all the Pinterest activity for your account.

However, managing all these different boards, and the comments and feedback you'll get, can be impossible.

And drive you insane.

One solution that REALLY took my Pinterest marketing to the next level was to "assign" different boards in my account to people within my "inner circle."

These can be:

- Employees
- Spouses
- Kids
- Cousins
- Neighbors

I asked three of my cousins — ages 14-18 — to handle a couple of my boards for me, just pin a couple items a day, and they LOVED it!

They were already on Pinterest and this made them feel very grown up.

Not only that, but they became very invested in my board, and my business, and had tons of great ideas on how to reach more people.

Leave it to a 15-year-old to hand me some of my best marketing ideas!

Funneling out work like this can keep your boards well-maintained, and your business thriving. (And as a bonus it gave me something to talk about at family holidays.)

Step No.4: Build Sneaky Backlinks Back to Your Boards

So, bear with me for just a moment, but I will get geeky. And that is: I'm gonna talk about "website backlinks."

Now, in the (somewhat) seedy world of Internet search engines, "backlinks" are links or bookmarks pointing to a specific webpage. Here, your Pinterest pinboards.

And any Internet search-engine guru worth their weight in Google salt would tell you "backlinks" are spammy and they can HURT the page you're trying to help.

Such as your own blog.

And this is true: except HUGE platforms such as Pinterest or Facebook are so powerful - way more powerful than your blog - that backlinks won't hurt at all.

In fact, they'll provide a huge boost to your pinboard's discover-ability.

So, how do you use "sneaky backlinks" to help the visibility of your pinboards? Well, here's the process I use each time:

1. **Make a list of the most important (and profitable) pinboards** in your own account. (Include the URL.)

2. **Head over to the freelance marketplace Fiverr and purchase an SEO "link pyramid" gig for five dollars.** Just type in "link pyramid" in the search bar and find a high-rated seller offering their services.

3. **Send the freelancer the URL of your pinboard**, along with the KEYWORD or KEYWORDS associated to that pinboard.

4. **Wait a couple weeks and watch your**

pinboard ZOOM up the search-engine ranks.

Now this strategy won't lead to INSTANT results. And it won't help a pinboard that has NO activity.

But if you're patient and you do this for a couple of your most important boards, you'll find a whole new swath of folks finding your pinboards.

Not just from Pinterest but from ALL over the Internet.

Chapter 4 Action Steps:

- **Come up with a list of 4-5 different boards you could create**. Product categories, holiday themes and behind-the-scenes stuff works best.

- **Create your boards and name them**. Keywords are powerful here, just make sure they sound interesting and original to humans.

- **Develop a Pinboard team**. Try to find members of your inner circle — friends and family work great here — that can help maintain some of your boards. This reduces your workload and gives you fresh ideas for your Pinterest marketing.

- **Buy a couple of backlinks for your pinboards**. Just head over to Fiverr and get a couple of "link pyramid" gigs to boost the discover-ability of your boards.

Chapter 5:

The How, What, Where and When of Pinterest Pins

"When one tugs at a single thing in nature, he finds it attached to the rest of the world."

-John Muir

Now we get to the fun part. We get to go a-pinning! (I've always wanted to say that.)

The actual mechanics of HOW to pin — which we'll go over in this chapter — is relatively simple. (It just takes a simple click.)

But WHAT to pin, and the best WHEN to pin and WHERE to send people to when they check out your pin, is more nuanced, and can derail your Pinterest marketing efforts quicker than a spilled latte on your laptop.

So, in this chapter I will walk you step-by-step through the art of pinning awesomeness.

And help you steer clear of some Pinterest marketing mistakes I made.

Quick note: When in doubt, just pin something. It's always better to pin too much, than not pin at all.

Pinning Pillar No.1: The HOW

As we discussed in an earlier chapter, there are four different ways to pin a photo or video:

- Click a "Pin It" button on a particular website
- Use the Pinterest bookmarklet browser extension (That funky icon in the upper-right of your Internet browser)
- Upload a photo or video to Pinterest
- Paste a specific URL into your Pinterest share dashboard

I use them all though I don't use the last one

very much. (Maybe I'm lazy.)

Of the four, I'd say my go-to tools are the "Pin It" button (most of the websites I visit have these icons all over them) AND the bookmarklet.

The bookmarklet, in case you're not up on your weird tech-y lingo, is a small icon that sits in the upper-right-hand corner of your web browser.

Having the bookmarklet makes it SUPER EASY to pin anything you come across in your web surfing travels.

One quick note: if you upload a photo or video to Pinterest — and there may be a time you want to do this — make sure the photo or video file name is a keyword.

So instead of having your photo or video named "Photo_1," you should instead name it something like "Decorative_Halloween_Candles," or something like that. This can make a big difference in the pin's ability to get discovered by the search engines.

Pinning Pillar No.2: The WHAT

This was the biggest question I had when getting started with Pinterest…what the heck do I fill all those boards up with?

Well, there's no hard-fast rule about this, but here's the advice I was given by a friend of mine, Michael Clarke, who runs the blog over at Punk Rock Marketing (reprinted with permission):

"Half (50%) of your pins should be re-pins, or simple pins of other stuff people have pinned. This will help you get more followers."

"A quarter (25%) of your pins should be interesting videos, pictures, resources — related to your field of crafty endeavor — that you did not create. (This would include things like blog posts, YouTube videos, funny viral memes you came across.)

"And (25%) of your pins should be YOUR own stuff — photos and videos, whatever you feel like will best show your awesome products."

Considering that nearly 85% of all Pinterest pins are people sharing other people's pins, this ratio will help you stand out in the Pinterest community with original pin content, but still keep you engaged with your followers and fans.

So, the next inevitable question is…where do we find all this cool stuff to pin?

Well, here's my little personal cheat sheet of places I like to go to find pin-worthy content.

Pin Source 1 - Sharing Other People's Stuff

This one's easy. Just head over to the good old Pinterest search bar and put in keywords related to your particular Etsy area.

There you'll find plenty of folks who are ALREADY big fans of the stuff you create. By pinning their stuff, they are much more likely to "follow" your own boards and may even end up buying some of your products.

One thing I recommend you do, though, is not SIMPLY put in a search term like "Etsy" and start repinning. (This will get you the notice of other Etsy sellers, which may or may not be a good strategy for you.)

Instead "think" like your ideal customer.

On one of our shops we sell "steampunk jewelry" - so we aren't just looking for other folks who sell the same stuff. We're trying to capture "steampunk fans."

That means repinning stuff from people who are fans of:

- Doctor Who
- Steampunk furniture
- Steampunk novels
- Jules Verne
- H.G. Wells
- Steampunk musicians (yes, there is such a good thing)
- Steampunk conventions
- Steampunk costumes

But you could do the same with shabby chic furniture. Or decorative soaps. Or Picasso-inspired Christmas ornaments.

Remember your product is tied to a larger creative aesthetic. (Find that aesthetic and you'll find a rich collection of would-be customers.)

Pin Source 2 - Interesting Photos/Videos

Well, this will depend on what particular slice of the Etsy pie you devour. But for me, here are my absolute go-to resources I check for stuff to pin:

- Facebook - By checking out what my extended Facebook network is sharing, I can get good ideas of what people might find interesting.

- AllTop - This is an interesting site where human beings - not machines, actual human beings -collect the best blog posts on a specific topic. (Chances are your area of emphasis is represented here somewhere.)

- YouTube - Most of the stuff on here is junk, but if I type in relevant keywords to my business, along with the words "how to," I'm likely to find something I can share with my Pinterest community.

- 500px - I found this photo site and I have to say…it's a-mazing! They collect high-res, breathtaking photos from around the world. (Won't have much to do with your Etsy shop, but it's always good to throw in these kinds of beautiful, motivational images from time to time.)

Pin Source 3 - Your Own Stuff

We went over this in Chapter 3, but this is where you get to show off your creative and visual flair — or at least the flair of your photographic assistant — by posting all the great images and videos related to your business.

The stuff that has done the best for me has been:

- Pets
- Kids

- Products
- Images of my workspace
- Behind-the-scenes videos
- A collage-like pin that contains all the product categories on offer (Like those old Sears Roebuck catalogs)
- Testimonial quotes from customers (usually as an overlay over a pretty picture)
- Anything that SCREAMS creativity

The better and crisper you can make your photos, the more they'll be shared. (And the more traffic they'll send back to your Etsy store.)

Which brings us to an important question: how do we make our photos ready for Pinterest prime-time?

Well, I've already shared my favorite FREE photo-editing tool, PicMonkey. It's the secret sauce to getting my photos cropped and looking their best.

But here's a couple things to keep in mind when getting your pics ready:

- **I've found the ideal photo size for Pinterest is 736x1128.** Go even taller than that, but your photo should be AT LEAST that big - and have that skyscraper ratio for maximum share-a-bility.

- **Play around with "saturation" filters.** PicMonkey, like many photo-editing tools out there, gives you a lot of cool filtration options. Current data suggests that adding saturation to your photos - making them brighter and more vivid - can boost engagement rates.

- **Add a text overlay (if relevant.)** A text overlay is a block of text displayed over an image. (Usually with some kind of textured background.) You may not always want to do this. But if you can, with your product images, I recommend it. It can make your images stand out in the crowded Pinterest sea and help people understand what they're looking at.

- **Don't put a PRICE in your text overlay.** I learned this the hard way, but you don't want to limit the price of your product inventory by putting it in the image. (Text caption is fine - those are easy to change - but not the overlay.) Just keep it simple…tell people what they're looking at.

Pinning Pillar No.3: The WHERE

So, finding the image or video to pin and add to your pinboard is just the first step. The real magic, for us Etsians, is in the caption.

Because it's in the caption, we can do important things such as:

- Add a link to our Etsy store and/or blog
- Insert Google-friendly keywords
- Include a call-to-action (CTA) to get people to take an action we'd like
- Add the price of a specific product featured in the pin

Obviously, the last one won't be relevant for every single pin you do. But as much as possible, it's key to hit as many of these objectives as you can.

Here's how I go about writing a description:

- **Start off with a brief, keyword-rich description of the pin image** - "Here's a vintage wooden dollhouse we built using aged timber…"

- **Add the call to action** - "To see our entire vintage dollhouse collection click here…."

- **Insert the product link** (include the whole URL; no URL shortening) - http://vintagedollhouse101.com

- **Include price, if relevant** (type out the dollar sign) - "$97"

- **Include ONE hashtag (of your business)** - Do not go overboard with hashtags. I know what the blog and the gurus say. But they are not a good long-term strategy. (Sends traffic to other sellers and Pinterest frowns on them.)

Now the CTA will change, depending on where you're sending people. (Maybe it's a "Sign up for email specials" or "Get 25% off our entire store.")

Regardless of the CTA, stick with this formula and it'll ensure your pins are focused, consistent and effective.

Pinning Pillar No.4: The WHEN

So when is the best time to do your pinning? Whenever you are most likely to reach your ideal audience.

When I first started out, I figured early morning would be the best. Eh...not so much! Turns out, as the day goes on, people use Pinterest as these little bits of mental vacation.

In my experience, I have found late afternoon (230-430 pm, EST) and evening (730 pm - 1130pm, EST) to be the best times to pin.

But this doesn't mean it will be the best for you. A couple things to keep in mind:

- **Where is most of your customer base**

located? I ship a ton to the East coast, so this is where I'm focused. But you may have a different audience.

- **Are there particular times when your audience stays off Pinterest?** Our shop sells to young moms, so the dinner family time is a dead zone. (But after the kids go to bed…"it's on!") But if you were catering to urban singles, you might find success elsewhere on the clock.

- **When are you MOST likely to be pinning?** There's no sense in creating an ideal pin schedule unless you, or somebody on your team, will stay committed to it. Figure out a time that works for you…and then test until you find the secret pinning sauce.

Chapter 5 Action Steps:

- **The HOW -** Install the Pinterest bookmarklet to your web browser of choice to make your future pinning effortless.

- **The WHAT -** Strive for a pinning mix of 25% repins, 25% external sources — such as YouTube, blog posts — and 50% photos of your Etsy products. And don't forget, for images to *a) Make 'em 736 x 1128* (A tool like PicMonkey makes this easier) *b) Experiment with saturation* and other filters *c) Add a text overlay description d) Don't put a price in the text image* overlay. (Learn from my mistakes!)

- **The WHERE -** For each pin caption, include a keyword-laden description of the image, a text call-to-action language and a link to your Etsy store or website.

- **The WHEN -** Pin in the late afternoon and evening, then try different times to see what gets the most engagement.

Chapter 6:

5 Ways to Get Hundreds of Followers in No Time

"A good friend is a connection to life - the key to sanity in a totally insane world."

-Lois Wyse

If you implement the strategies I've outlined in this book so far, then you'll already attract some Pinterest buzz and boost your follower count.

But if you want to make a dent with your Pinterest marketing, you will need to take it up a notch…that's what we will cover in this chapter.

I'm going over my top five strategies for getting tons of Pinterest followers — without having to pay a single dime. (I go over more advanced, paid options for boosting your Pinterest presence in Chapter 7.)

Just remember that Rome wasn't built in a day, and neither was your Pinterest platform. Building followers takes time.

But if you stick with it, and use these six follower techniques, you'll have a Pinterest army of fans and customers before you know it!

Follower Strategy No.1: Find (and Follow) Your Future Customers

Having used all the social media platforms out there — even Myspace, what a mistake that was — I can say I LOVE the Pinterest search engine.

Most social networks, like Twitter and Facebook, make it hard to find individuals interested in what you have to sell.

But, because of the themed-board nature of Pinterest, finding those future purveyors of your Etsy wares is super easy.

All you gotta do is:

- Type in a keyword, related to your business, in the Pinterest search field
- Select "Pinners" tab
- Then follow all the "pinners" who've pinned good stuff related to that keyword

I find about 60% of the people I follow will follow me back. (Which is great!)

And they are some of the most engaged Pinterest friends I've got. (Because I already know my stuff is a great fit with their personality.)

This can also apply to "boards." Do a keyword search — filter it by boards — and you'll find a whole treasure trove of boards that are just waiting to be followed. (Believe me, Pinterest is so new you'll have great success with this technique.)

Follower Strategy No.2: Share the Pinterest Love

One other great way to build up your follower base is to pin other people's pins. There's nothing people like more than recognition, and a couple of well-placed pins could get you the attention of some serious Pinterest heavyweights…who could then turn into customers.

Besides, getting noticed on Pinterest by an Etsy store owner is one of the biggest compliments a Pinterest user can get. (Crazy, right?)

So…don't worry about pinning other people stuff too much. It's great for your platform and can put money in your pocket.

And don't forget the same TIME recommendations for "pinning" also apply to "repinning."

For me the golden repinning times are early afternoon (about 2:30 p.m. EST) and early evening (8:00 p.m. EST).

But experiment until you find what works for you.

Follower Strategy No.3: Comment and Engage With Popular Pins

This is a very effective method overlooked by many business folks marketing on Pinterest. (And not just us Etsy types.)

Pinterest has this interesting area where they collect the most popular pins. And so all you need to do is pick out a few of these each day and leave some kind of comment.

Now, try to make it a constructive comment. Not…"nice"…or "cool!"

Write something interesting, like: "I have an Argentinian Mountain Llama with the same name!" or…"Sure I wore matching denim to my sophomore dance…"

Believe me, these are SEEN by tons of people, and if it's a pin that's focused in an area that has overlap with your business you'll get some much-needed eyeballs.

Follower Strategy No.4: Add Pinterest Icons to Your Website

If you've got a blog or a website, and I hope you do, one of the best things you can do to amass your collection of Pinterest fanatics is to adorn your site with:

- **Pinterest buttons:** These are the ones that let people pin any image on your website.
- **Follow Me Buttons:** These are the buttons that let people follow you on Pinterest, right there from your site.

To install the buttons on your site head over to the Pinterest button page. They have a great tutorial there and they walk you through it step-by-step.

Now, if you have no web presence, other than your Etsy store, then this won't be a super-helpful option.

But if you have any kind of website or blog

going, and you've got a ton of pictures on there, then this simple marketing tweak can increase your Pinterest follower count by as much as 40-50%. (I know it did for me.)

Follower Strategy No.5: Promote Your Pinterest Account…Everywhere!

Besides your blog or website, there are OTHER key places where you can promote your Pinterest account and they include:

- **Your Facebook page** (Just connect one of the app icons to your Pinterest account)
- **Your email signature**
- **Your YouTube channel** (If you have one)
- **Your Google + page and Tumblr blog** (Every one of my pins gets re-purposed on these two)
- **Your LinkedIn profile or company page**
- **Your Twitter account** (You can even get Twitter to auto-post your pins for you)

- **Anywhere else** you can think of

I know this may seem like a lot of work - but most of this stuff is very "set it and forget it." And it can bang the promotional drum for you (without you have to do much.)

Follower Strategy No.6: Pin as Much as You Can

Nothing earth-shattering here. The more you pin, the more followers you get.

This doesn't you mean have to spend 18 hours a day filling up your boards. Just try to get into the habit of whenever you're surfing the web or doing anything with your favorite device — I love to do most of my pinning on my smartphone — try to be pinning at the same time.

It'll save you time and put you that much closer to your goal of some new cash flow into your Etsy business.

And if you can't seem to get yourself motivated

to do much pinning - and we all hit that at some point - try to view your "pinning" as research. (I can't tell you how many cool, interesting ideas I've gotten from cruising around Pinterest looking for interesting things to pin.)

Chapter 6 Action Steps:

- **Follow Pinterest users who represent your ideal customers**. Use keywords to find Pinterest users who have pins and/or boards related to your Etsy product offerings.

- **Pin, or repin, other pins to connect with new followers**. Most users will feel flattered and follow you back.

- **Comment on the most popular pins.** Say something witty and/or constructive to open your follower base to a whole new slice of the Pinterest community.

- **Add Pinterest icons to your website**. Insert code onto your website or blog to make sure each of your images have the "Pin It" icon overlay, and that visitors can follow you on Pinterest, from your website.

- **Pin as much as you can**. More Pinterest activity = more followers.

Chapter 7:

Zen and the Art of the

Pinterest Contest

"Life is more fun if you play games."

Roald Dahl

This is the part of Pinterest that is exciting.

Because nothing, and I mean nothing, can increase your number of Pinterest followers and send a crazy amount of traffic to your Etsy store…

Like a good old Pinterest contest. (Not to mention get you some FREE press if you play your cards right.)

Now, not all Pinterest contests are created equal; I've created my fair share of turkeys that did little more than clog up my inbox.

But if you follow these simple steps and leverage your existing your network to help get the word about your contest, then you have a fantastic chance of doubling, or tripling, your revenue in a matter of a week.

Ready to become a Pinterest contest expert?

Pinterest Contest Tip No.1: Stay Behind the White Line

As effective as Pinterest contests are, there's been a lot of abuse from less-then scrupulous marketers using them for nefarious means.

And Pinterest, trying to avoid some growing pains that afflicted Facebook and Twitter, have tried their best to rein in some contest craziness.

So, before you create your contest, realize you CANNOT ask people, as a condition of entry, to:

- Pin the rules of your contest
- Pin any promotional material related to your

contest

- Pin an image, or set of images, that you designate
- Vote for winners with pins or likes

And the big-mongo No-No is to insinuate that Pinterest endorses your contest.

I know you've seen Pinterest contests run, maybe even recently, that used some of the above strategies. And what you do in your corner of the Pinterest world is your business, however...

I think Pinterest marketing is a long-term strategy and I would hate to see any of my Craft Biz aficionados get their account suspended or ended due to a simple contest oversight.

Pinterest Contest Tip No.2: Set the Ground Rules for the Contest

Here's where you get to let your creative juices flow. You could do a contest about almost anything:

- Have entrants upload a photo or video that

is the most funny/creative/whacky…..something!

- Have entrants do a virtual scavenger hunt where they have to look for clues in your various boards.

- Have entrants create the most imaginative and interesting board they can think of (based on a theme you come up with)

- Have entrants vote on the name, style, color, size or design of your latest creation. (The winner gets it FREE!)

- Have entrants choose a favorite product between 2-4 choices. (The winner goes on SALE!)

The key thing is to determine whether you are doing a sweepstake — where the winner is chosen at random — or a merit-based contest where the BEST (whatever) wins.

I've done both, and I like both. But anything that encourages the Pinterest community to be creative gets them very involved. (And willing to share it with their social network.)

Note: You CAN make being a follower of you or one of your boards be a condition of the contest…you can't make it the ONLY condition.

Pinterest Contest Tip No.3: Pick a Really Good Prize

Don't be cheap here. Don't just give away one of your $10 ornaments. You want it to be something cool. And interesting.

Maybe it's one of your nice products. Or maybe it's some kind of artisan tool, or rare book or neat collectible you know your ideal audience would be interested in.

Try to avoid the boring, generic iPad or Kindle. (You'll get a bunch of freeloaders who have no interest in your Etsy merchandise.)

One REALLY cool thing I've done is to offer a Skype tutorial where I walk somebody how to create one of my offerings.

Don't worry, they won't be a competitor.

It can be a cool way to generate buzz and make a customer for life.

Pinterest Contest Tip No.4: Set a Time Limit

I generally like to go about a week for my contests. I've also done as little as three or four days. (Really depends on how the nice the prize is.)

Trust me: you don't want to go more than a week. People will get antsy and it will kill the urgency of the contest.

However long you make the contest, try to have the contest end on Sunday night. This way you'll take advantage of all that awesome weekend traffic to boost the number of entrants.

Pinterest Contest Tip No.5: Bring in the Big Guns

I need to be honest. Running a Pinterest contest is a real pain in the butt. Which is why I don't run it.

I use a service called WishPond. They handle all the things I don't want to.

Such as:

- Creating entry forms
- Generating templates for your blog or website
- Making sure the contest meets U.S. contest guidelines (A much bigger deal than you'd think)
- Making sure all the contest landing pages are mobile-friendly
- Providing tons of promotional tools you can use on Twitter and Facebook
- Helping me schedule the contest (so I don't have to be there)
- Producing reports so I know how successful the contest is
- Setting up the follow-email sequence for everyone who enters

I swear, I'd pay 10 times what I do for the

WishPond service. It's that good.

But if you're on a super tight budget, they've got a 7-day FREE trial which you could try out and do a super mini-contest to see how it goes.

I know there are other services and applications that help you run Pinterest contests, but I haven't used them, so I can't endorse any.

Whatever you do, don't run it yourself. You'll drive yourself — and your Pinterest community — crazy.

Pinterest Contest Tip No.6: Promote the Heck Out of Your Contest

After I've set up the basics of my contest, it's time to tell everybody about your contest.

This includes:

- Facebook friends and family
- Facebook fans (If you have a Fan Page)
- Twitter followers
- Pinterest followers (Duh!)

- Fellow Etsy forum members
- Email subscribers
- Total strangers you meet on the street

And doing these will spread the message. But here are a couple extra ways to take that contest promotion to the major leagues:

- Create a Facebook ad campaign
- Buy a couple of sponsored tweets (Focus on followers of the Etsy twitter account)
- Send out a press release
- Buy ad space in any newsletters or weekly emails focused on your ideal customer

I have to say, Facebook ads are my biggest driver of traffic to my contest page.

And every time I run a contest which is about once every couple months — don't want to overdo it — I see a huge bump in sales, email subscribers and repeat business.

And repeat business is where the REAL money is.

Chapter 7 Action Steps:

- **Familiarize yourself with what you can — and can't — do with a Pinterest contest.** Be sure entrants don't have to pin specific images to qualify — and never imply Pinterest endorses your contest.

- **Determine what entrants must do to enter the contest.** This can include voting on products, creating a board or uploading a photo or video related to a theme you create.

- **Decide on a cool contest prize.** Don't be cheap, but don't make it generic — like an iPad or Kindle.

- **Let a Pinterest contest app service, such as WishPond, handle the details.** Running a contest is a royal pain; you don't want to sweat the small stuff.

- **Promote your contest in as many ways as you can.** This includes Facebook, Twitter, online ad campaigns, email newsletters and (even) press releases.

Chapter 8:

How to Get a Ph.D. in

Pinterest Marketing Studies

"I never let my schooling get in the way of my education."
Mark Twain

Okay, maybe not a Ph.D. But certainly a Masters, at the very least.

That's because the tips, tricks, tools and apps I'm going to go over in this chapter are a bit more on the advanced side.

That doesn't mean they a require a 4.0 GPA and 12 units of Algebra. But it does mean that they are best done after you have some Pinterest marketing experience under your belt.

If only to find out whether you enjoy this

Pinterest thing anyway.

So, let's jump right in with my 5-6-4 Tools for Advanced Pinterest Domination:

Tool #1: Canva

Someone perusing the boards dedicated to my Etsy shop might believe I have a team of graphic designers working around-the-clock to produce my Pinterest pins.

Oh, if only that were the case.

Instead I use the powerful (and mostly-free) Canva app. Started by Melanie Perkins, one of the youngest female CEOs in the world, this service allows you to generate professional-looking pin images – along with a whole host of other things – in just a couple clicks.

The best part about Canva, besides the cool selection of pre-made templates is that you don't have to THINK about things like pixel sizes. (They've got all that figured out for you.)

All you have to do is click on "Pinterest" under

social media templates, drag over a design you like, and start creating your masterpiece.

The only downside is you can get lost in a bit of a time suck going through all the creative options. (I suggest you set a strict time limit on how long you'll spend on your images.)

Another tip is, when promoting content – if you do create content – is to create a standard "look and feel" of how you'll promote all your blog posts and videos.

Don't try to come up with a unique image for each. (That's what your product stills are for.)

But instead come up with a no-brainer, copy-and-paste template that can let you churn out pins quickly and effectively.

Tool #2: Tailwind

If there's one big "pain" to the whole Pinterest marketing side of things, it's that it requires a lot of scheduling, and often at inopportune times for a human.

That's why the Tailwind tool is so cool.

For just $10/month, you can schedule your Pinterest pins weeks, if not months, in advance. Or you can just set it up that pins get published in the next available queue.

Why this is so powerful is that you dial it down to the very minute, such as 4:34 pm on Thursday.

Now, this advanced tool probably won't do you much good until you're publishing at least 3-5 pins a day. Less than that and it'll be a waste of time.

But whether you do it yourself, or hand it off to an assistant, this tool can help keep your Pinterest content on schedule…even when you aren't.

Tool #3: Ninja Pinner

Don't let the somewhat obnoxious name fool you.

Ninja Pinner is a great little piece of software that lets you follow – and unfollow – targeted

Pinterest users in the background, all while you focus on more important things.

Like getting those glue gun burns patched up on your fingers.

I generally like to target users based on whether they follow certain boards or whether they have repined or liked a certain pin. (I can even focus it by search results.)

And then I just let the software do its thing. (And that thing includes unfollowing people who don't follow you back and automatically repining and liking, if you want.)

Kind of like having your very own Pinterest virtual assistant. (And luckily this is one assistant who won't leave a mess in the office kitchen.)

Tool #3: IFTTT (If This, Then That)

If you haven't heard of this FREE tool, then let me introduce you to your new lifesaver…IFTTT.

This free app lets you create automated workflows based on connecting various and diverse systems.

For example, on Pinterest, I have it set up that:

- I publish a tweet every time a new pin is published
- All my Instagram posts get re-purposed on Pinterest
- All my new pin images get archived in a folder on my Facebook photo album

But I use it for a lot of other cool things in life. (Like sending me a text message when a family member is within three miles of the house.)

All in all a great addition to not only your marketing toolbox, but your overall Etsian life.

Tool #4: Pin Groupie

Don't worry.

No one is going to ask you to quit your Etsy career and go follow Jimmy Buffet on tour.

But this tool allows you to leverage a powerful though somewhat hard-to-crack promotional tool.

Pinterest groups.

The cool part about Pinterest groups is that they are a bit of a captive audience.

The not-so-cool part is it's hard to find those groups.

Until now.

PinGroupie allows you to hone in on exactly the type of potential customers you want. They have over 30 categories to choose from. And a search engine which lets you scour the groups for keywords related to your Etsy slice of the world.

It's also FREE, which is nice.

Not as nice as 2 free front-row tickets to a Jimmy Buffet concert.

But nice nonetheless.

Chapter 8 Action Steps:

- **Try Canva to make your Pinterest images pop**. Forget the expensive graphic designers or hours spent learning Photoshop. Play with the pin templates on Canva…but don't play too long.

- **Schedule your pins in advance with Tailwind**. Post your pins in advance, in the afternoon and evenings, without hunkering over your computer all day. (Best when you're producing at least 2-3 pins a day.)

- **Give IFTTT a spin**. Not just for marketing stuff. But life stuff. It's that good.

- **Become a PinGroupie.** Use PinGroupie to get the lowdown on groups you should join and participate in. You might even find a group dedicated to Etsy-lovin' Jimmy Buffet fans!

Chapter 8:

How to Get a Ph.D. in Pinterest Marketing Studies

"I never let my schooling get in the way of my education."
Mark Twain

Congratulations!

If you've made it this far, then you officially have a masters degree in Pinterest Studies, from the University of Craft Biz Insider. (Diplomas available in the lobby.)

Here's the crazy thing: Pinterest is so NEW nobody knows — not all those social media experts and Pinterest fanatics or even the CEO of Pinterest — what the future holds for this company.

Some people think it's just a flash in the pan. Other people think it will surpass Facebook as the dominant social network.

For me, it's not about whether Pinterest will stay

around long enough to go public and make their investors billions of dollars.

It's about realizing that Pinterest represents a huge change in the way we communicate and connect with the people in our lives — and the companies that sell the stuff we want.

That it's all about telling a story with a picture. Conveying your company's mission statement in a single product still. Getting the world to stop and pay attention...with only a 500px image at your disposal.

The cool, awesome, amazing thing is, as Etsy sellers, we are poised to take massive advantage of this opportunity. Not just to sell more stuff and make more money.

But to champion a belief that crafts that are made in a barn in Pennsylvania, or in a craft room in Portland are far better than some factory-made rip-off produced in a factory in China.

So, as you give the tactics in this book a try, resist the urge to get bogged down in the details.

Procedures could change, guidelines could be altered, or the method of any individual social network could undergo a transformation overnight.

But what won't change is the power these social networks give our customers to express themselves through the images they pin — and the handmade artisans they support.

And that's something Wal-Mart can never do.

Oh, and one more thing before I go...

•

A Special FREE Gift for You!

If you'd like FREE instant access to my special report "Top 10 Marketing Tools Every Etsy Seller Should Use" then head over to **CraftBizInsider.com/Free**.

(What else you gonna do? Watch another "Twilight" movie?!)

Grab the Entire "Selling On Etsy Made Easy" Collection!

How to Sell on Etsy With Facebook

How to Sell on Etsy With Blogging

How to Sell on Etsy With Instagram

DISCLAIMER AND/OR LEGAL NOTICES: